Midas Mindset for Gentepreneurs:

How to Turn Your Thoughts into Gold, Success and Happiness

Marcos Orozco

Midas Mindset for Gentepreneurs

Copyright © 2015 Marcos Orozco

All rights reserved. This book may not be reproduced in any form, in whole or in part (beyond the copying permitted by U.S. Copyright Law, Section 107, "fair use" in teaching or research, Section 108, certain library copying, or in published media by reviewers in limited excerpts), without written permission from the author.

This book is licensed for your personal enjoyment only. This book may not be resold or given away. Thank you for respecting the hard work of the author.

Disclaimer

While best efforts have been used, the author is not offering legal, accounting, medical, or any other professional services advice and makes no representations or warranties of any kind and assume no liabilities of any kind with respect to the accuracy or completeness of the contents and specifically disclaim any implied warranties of merchantability or fitness of use for a particular purpose, nor shall the author be held liable or responsible to any person or entity with respect to any loss or incidental or consequential damages caused, or alleged to have been caused, directly or indirectly, by the information or programs contained herein. The views expressed are those of the author alone, and should not be taken as expert instruction or commands. The reader is responsible for his or her own actions. Adherence to all applicable laws and regulations, including international, federal, state, and local governing professional licensing, business practices, advertising, and all other aspects of doing business in the United States or any other jurisdiction is the sole responsibility of the purchaser or reader. Neither the author nor the publisher assumes any responsibility or liability whatsoever on the behalf of the purchaser or reader of these materials.

ISBN-13:9781514820766

ISBN-10:1514820765

▶ Dedication

Dedicated to those who are no longer with us. Thank you for the memories and know your departure from this physical world is not in vain.

Eric Orozco

Armando and Leo Bermudez

Albert Medrano

Walter Paredes

Gabriel Matamoros

Matt Hamm

Jason Neal

Sasha Mata

Daniel "Tantrum"

Brian "Zeres" Stains

David "Anger" Ybarra

Eddie "Smokey" Casillas

Raymond and his younger brother

Bernie Aka Blinky

Loe One

Craig Asmah

Baby Blue

Near One, Carlos Lopez

▶ Contents

▶ Dedication v

▶ Acknowledgments ix

▶ Introduction 1

▶ 1 À La Carte Personality 5

▶ 2 Environment for Success 13

▶ 3 Become Intentional with Life 23

▶ 4 Daily Success Habits 31

▶ 5 Fail Forward toward Success 39

▶ 6 Progress vs. Perfection 47

▶ 7 Making Decisions with Core Values 55

▶ 8 Leadership Starts with You 61

- ▶ | 9 Abundant Mindset 67
- ▶ | 10 How to Manifest Your Thoughts into Reality 75
- ▶ | 11 Stop Judging People 85
- ▶ | 12 Balance Is for Circus Animals 93
- ▶ | 13 Two Types of Motivation 99
- ▶ | 14 Identity Yourself 107
- ▶ | 15 Invest in Yourself 115
- ▶ | 16 Meditate Vs. Medicate 125
- ▶ | 17 My Five Daily Rituals to Success 131
- ▶ | About the Author 143
- ▶ | Thank You 145
- ▶ | Connect with Me 147

▶ Acknowledgments

I would like to dedicate this book to my son Noah who inspires me daily. I would also like to thank my parents Marlene and Marcos Orozco who gave me the tools to develop my moral character. They taught me core values that have allowed me to be successful. Without these values, I would not be here writing this book. I want to thank all of my family, and friends who support and believed in me since day one. I also want to thank all of my mentors and all of you who have inspired me in different ways! Les Brown, Grant Cardone, Jim Rohn, Gary Vaynerchuck, Mike Koenigs, Pam Hendrickson, Russell Brunson, Wayne Dyer, Anthony Robins, John Maxwell, Daewon Song, Carlos Torres, Violet Brown, Myles Kovacs, Daymond John, Manny and Angela Ruiz, Nely Galan, Francisco Cortes, Gaby Natale, Mia Perez,

Marcos Orozco

John Lee Dumas, Don Tolman, Larry Broughton, Angelica Perez Litwin and Latinas Think Big Network, Emma Tiebens, Ruben Mata, Michael Stevenson, Joel Bauer, Michael Hyatt, Angelica Urquijo, Michelle Patterson, David Fagan, Davi and ALEGRIA Magazine, George Urban Jibaro Torrez, Jose Salcedo, Michele Ruiz, Hugo Balta, Pedro Quiroba Mr. Latino Magazine, Rikki Rincon, Arturo Nava, Steve Gallegos, Carla Sanchez Anderson, Ovidilio Vasquez, Victor Palomares, Meg Le Vu, Coach Damiano, Michelle Patterson, Eddie Velez, Mario Lopez, Armando Bermudez, Benny Juarez, Jeannette Sandoval, Patty Dominguez, Case Vera, Adam Farhat, Eddie Castillo, Victor Glez, Adam Flores, Christopher Zapien, Maudie and Karen Orozco, Lisa Marie, Peggy Sullivan, Shereen Faltas, Deborah Deras, Preston Smiles, Alexi Panos, Raquel Cordoba, Belinda Arlington, Eiji Morishita, Cecilia Lopez, Eric Maier and family, Tia Flori, Tio Arnold, Enrique Ferrufino, and everyone who I had the pleasure to cross paths with, forgive me if I didn't mention you including all of my fellow **Gentepreneurs** making things happen, I wish you incredible success!

▶ Introduction

This is supposed to be the "Introduction." They tell me that I'm supposed to write something that compels you to read this book. I've decided to do things differently. I'm going to be 100% transparent and speak from the heart.

I would like to clear the air. I'm not an Academic Scholar, a PHD or even a professional psychologist. Heck, I don't even consider myself a writer. I'm a regular person just like you—Imperfect in many ways.

I was compelled to share with you some of the lesson that I learned along my personal journey. I went from planning my own funeral at the age of 17 years old, homeless and depressed to generating millions of dollars in revenue for my business ventures and my clients.

It took me a lifetime and a fortune to learn the golden lessons that I share with you in this book. I've done many things right, and I've also failed in many ways, but the lessons you learn about yourself are more valuable than gold. Maybe my parents were right—I love to learn the hard way. The key words here are "love to learn." I'm a student of success; I'm a student of life. These Midas Mindset lessons are priceless to me. I couldn't see myself trading them for a Billion dollars.

So imagine having the power to turn your thoughts into Gold, Success and Happiness. The good news is that it's possible. Anything and everything is just a thought away. If I can do it, so can you. Looking back, it's rather simple once you make the decision to believe you are worthy. The mere fact that you are reading this book proves you are on the right path. I believe in you. See you at the top!

Disclaimer: Thank you for reading this book. English is my second language and I don't consider myself a "writer". I do consider myself a student of life and want to share with you valuable lessons that have changed my life. If you find any mistakes, **PLEASE** tell me by sending the error and page you found it on to my email **MidasMindset@gmail.com.** Thanks in advance.

This is an Interactive Book with Free Videos!

Please register by visiting the website, and get instant access to **17 FREE videos** that summarize each chapter. Simply go to:

www.MidasMindsetBook.com

or scan this QR code with your smartphone.

▶ | 1

À La Carte Personality

> *The "self-image" is the key to human personality and human behavior. Change the self-image and you change the personality and the behavior.*
>
> —Maxwell Maltz

Life is about making choices. Who and what you want to be is simply a choice. When I was young, about 12 years old, I remember watching one of those popular teenage movies at my friend's house then walking home all excited because the movie was cool, almost as if I was in the movie as one of the characters. I could still hear the theme song from the movie playing in my head. As I walked past a mirror in my house, I stopped and looked in; and I've got to tell you, I was highly disappointed.

I wasn't good looking like the staring cast in the movie. I didn't have colored eyes, I didn't have nice hair. As a matter of fact, my hair was dark and nappy. My nose was big and I had big ears. And then thought to myself, "I looked like a rodent." Why? Because my buddies in my baseball team used to call me rat boy because they said I looked like the character from that movie. And if that wasn't enough, I was always the shortest kid in school. I was highly disappointed because I didn't look like the starting cast in the movie.

I didn't like how I felt, from feeling unstoppable to feeling like I didn't belong and I felt ugly for the first time in my life. That's when I made a choice to have a heart to heart with myself. I said, "You know what? You're going to have to work extra-hard my dear friend, because your looks are average at best, and I'm being generous when I said average." This was the first time I had a talk with myself on a real level. I thought about it then continued. "You're going to have to develop an awesome personality. You're going to have to be funny. You're going to have to be smart and witty. You're going to have to be a man with charisma. You're going to have to be a gentleman with high integrity."

Then Instinctively I started thinking about people I wanted to mimic and internalize some of their character traits. I instantly thought about my dear mom. What do I love about my mom that I can mimic? I asked myself. I love the fact that she is a gentle and kind woman. She has a big heart. She cares about others and she never gives up. She was feminine yet powerful, I thought about this and internalized it. Then I thought about my father. What do I love about my father? What character traits could I borrow from him? My dad is an awesome individual. He is funny, he's a great storyteller, and he's a man of integrity. He works hard and he's very, very organized.

I internalized some of those traits; then I went on to take a look at other people, my teacher Mrs. Oreagan. What do I like about Mrs. favorite science teacher? I love the questions she asks. I love her curiosity and her ability to see the best in people. Then I look at characters on the big screen; what do I like about Ferris from *Ferris Bueller's Day Off*? Ferris I thought was cool so I wanted to internalize his wit, charismatic charm and connections. I was creating a stew of different personality traits that I wanted to integrate with mine.

What I started doing is identifying and choosing the personality I wanted to have. This didn't happen overnight. It took me years and years, but I learned at a young age that I was able to pick my personality and how I wanted to be. I started internalizing these character and personality traits, by closing my eyes and running random scenarios in my brain. I would act them out—how I wanted those scenarios to play out. How did I act in those scenarios? I would repeat this over and over and over and over again. Basically I was programming myself in these situations.

This is pretty much one of the most important things I have ever done. I didn't get better looking. I didn't get much taller. But I became many of the things I wanted to be. This is definitely one of the smartest and least expensive investments in my personal development and I started at a young age.

If you don't like certain things about yourself, you can change them! You can replace them. Find somebody in your life you would like to emulate, and then internalize it. Then begin by going through scenarios in your head. It's incredible how powerful your brain is, how you can reroute the way you think of yourself and how you act. It's very powerful tool.

Altering your personality is nothing new; shy people have been doing it for years, wishing for a more outgoing personality. Overly aggressive people may wish for the opposite. Experts in the field believe that changing patterns and certain habits and beliefs—the traits you don't find appealing to yourself—are crucial to personality change. First of all, how are personalities formed? By environment, upbringing, people in our lives, or experiences? It's actually a mixture of all of these. After all, we are a product of our environment. Genetics are of course important, but studies show that our upbringing and environment, etc., interact with our genetic blueprints and actually shape us.

▶ | Questions

1. You can change your personality if you want to: True or False

2. What would you change about your current personality?

3. Name a person who has a great personality trait that you can mimic.

_____

_____

_____

_____

_____

_____

_____

This is an Interactive Book with Free Videos!

Please register by visiting the website, and get instant access to **17 FREE videos** that summarize each chapter. Simply go to:

www.MidasMindsetBook.com

or scan this QR code with your smartphone.

► | Notes

_____

_____

_____

_____

▶ | 2

Environment for Success

We begin to see, therefore, the importance of selecting our environment with the greatest of care, because environment is the mental feeding ground out of which the food that goes into our minds is extracted.

—Napoleon Hill

When I was growing up in Gardena, California, I lived in an environment that was gang and drug infested. I witnessed drug transactions, gang activities, crime and graffiti everywhere. Even though I had great parents, at home they were not getting along and would argue often.

I took to the streets and eventually ended up hanging with the local knuckleheads. Eventually I excelled in this environment because as humans we adapt accordingly, and I thrive in competitive environments. Luckily for me, my parents gave me great moral foundation to reference and come back to.

Many of my friends didn't have two parents like I did and the troubled ones had something in common—their mothers were using heavy drugs. Many of my high school friends are still incarcerated and others never made it past their teen years. My environment was so toxic that I was planning my own funeral at the age of 17. I had a list of phone numbers hard written on a piece of paper for my mom to call and invite them to my funeral. I remember I wanted to have the biggest funeral, bigger than that of my friends who had already died. I even had a song picked out and I knew exactly what cemetery I wanted to be buried in. It wanted to be buried close to my friends so that they can come visit me at Roosevelt Memorial Park on Vermont in Gardena California. It was normal to get shot at in my city. Keep in mind; this was during the crack epidemic in Los Angeles and during the birth of Gangsta Rap in Los Angeles. It seemed as if the local gangs were in control of our street as they fought for drug turf.

This was a tough external environment. Most environmental issues are not zip code related; which means you can live in a rough area of town or city with delinquents around you, and still have a positive atmosphere. Your zip code is only a small percentage of your environment.

I would like to talk about internal environments, which are so important. Every time I hear the word environment I think about children, and I think about my youth and how I lived in a toxic environment, for the most part. It doesn't have to be that way.

Your home environment is the most important environment that you should focus on. I'm going to talk about what's surrounding us. If you're watching television, what are you watching? Are you watching the trashy news, where all they talk about is Global terrorism, financial meltdowns, Ebola and other pandemic breakouts for that month? Are you watching shows that bring no value? It's like junk food, empty calories for your mind. It brings no value to your life. They're nothing but gossip and sensationalism. If you or your kids are playing video games, are they constructive and good for your mental development? Or are they violent first person shooter games that seem to be so popular.

What kind of music are you listening to? Are you listening to adult themed music or songs about nonstop parties, drug use and violence? Are you listening to bad messages, or are you listening to something that inspires and moves you? What type of people are you hanging around with? That's another environmental issue. Are you hanging around with people who are always gossiping about others? If they're gossiping about others, what do you think they're doing when you're not there? Do you think you're the exception? You are probably the norm and they are talking about you too.

There's a great saying from the late Jim Rohn that says you are the average of the five people you hang around with. If you're hanging around with people who are just average and not going anywhere, not shooting for excellence and contribution to society then odds are you will become the average of those five people. If you want to find new, like-minded people, that is something you have to do. It doesn't mean you just cut people out of your life, unless they're really negative, but it means you need to find people who are better for your personal environment.

Also, for children in the school environment, you have to ask yourself, *what kind of kids are going to that school?* If you go to a public school, guess what, you have to work harder with your child most of the time. You have to be a bigger influence. You have to stack the cards in your favor for success, for a better environment. In my situation, when I spend time with my son, I consider it quality time. I don't have a television at home, so we don't sit around watching TV and there's only two types of music that I play for him; giving him the choice between classical or toddler music. Believe it or not, he loves the classical music.

In our personal environment we draw, we imagine, we play and we read. Reading is another environmental issue; what are you reading? Are you reading smut? Are reading gossip or are you reading something that enlightens you and brings you closer to your desires and your goals and your dreams? Now I don't have any gripes against music. I don't have any gripes against television, in moderation, but if you're doing it to distract you from the things you should be doing, then there's a problem there. Stack the cards in your favor. Change your environment and it'll start to pay off almost immediately. I challenge you to stop watching Television for 2 weeks and see how much more you get done.

▶ | **Questions**

1. How many hours of television do you watch each week?

2. How many hours a week do you read books?

3. What can you do right now to improve your environment?

_____

_____

_____

_____

_____

_____

_____

_____

_____

This is an Interactive Book with Free Videos!

Please register by visiting the website, and get instant access to **17 FREE videos** that summarize each chapter. Simply go to:

www.MidasMindsetBook.com

or scan this QR code with your smartphone.

▶ | Notes

_____

_____

_____

_____

Midas Mindset for Genteprenuers

▶ | 3

Become Intentional with Life

Our intention creates our reality.

—Wayne Dyer

Setting an intention in the morning, or the night before, can be magical. Let me share with you a quick story that happened to me. A couple of years ago I went through a breakup with my former fiancé. We decided to part ways and we were moving out of our house in Long Beach, I was moving to Manhattan Beach but I was going to live at my mom's house in Torrance for a couple of weeks. I was excited about it because she was going to soon retire to Nicaragua and it would be a good bonding experience for us. One gloomy Monday morning I had to finish moving out the entire garage from Long Beach to a local storage and a feeling of doom swept over me. I had a lot to move; a motorcycle, wakeboards, heavy boxes and several other things that I didn't want to leave behind.

That morning I remember thinking, "Man, today is going to suck major." I woke up in an ugly mood just thinking about what I had to do when all of a sudden I said to myself, "You know what? Today is going to be the best day ever." Knowing full well that thinking such a thing was nearly impossibility; pretty much not even possible for me. But I just set that intention out there—the first time I really set an intention like that.

I said, "You know what? Today is going to be the best day ever, and that's it." The more I thought that, the more I felt this intention grow. So I rented a U-Haul truck and drove it all the way to Long Beach. I started in the garage, moving the motorcycle, and with a little help from the neighbor, then I packed and moved all the boxes and the wakeboards.

Things were not going that well to be honest, but for some reason, I had a great attitude about it. Hours and hours had gone by while taking everything to storage. I returned the U-Haul truck and finally got back to my mother's house in Torrance around 11:00 p.m. I opened the door and saw that my mom was in her bedroom with the lights on, and she's reading her bible.

"Hi, Mom." It was late, so I was surprised that she was awake. I went over to her and sat down. "How was your day?" She asked.

"It was great. Not that bad." I replied. We started talking and were soon into a deep conversation. We talked for over 2 hours on the deepest level possible, mother and son; me as an adult and wiser individual going through transition. We connected like never before. It was one of the most incredible conversations I've ever had.

When I finally lay down to go to sleep, I realized that this day had been somewhat special. It was one of the best days ever!! All of a sudden, I remembered, wait a minute. I set that intention first thing that morning. I knew—by me setting that intention, it made all of this possible—so I changed my mind about how the day was going to go.

I verbally professed and said it was going to be the best day, and guess what, it was definitely one of the best days ever because I got to connect with my mom. By setting my intention, my day became better, things worked out and I felt better about everything.

Set an Intention and Activate It with Action!

Clarify your intent. When you wake up, what is it you want to experience for that day? What is the outcome you are looking for? There really is nothing that needs to be done, other than you stating your intention to yourself then acting to make it so; manifesting our intention. Focus on what you want to happen that day; what kind of day will you have, what is your goal? By manifesting this intent, you are absorbing it into your being. We get what we manifest and more.

The more passion and emotional energy we can put into our desire; the greater our ability to create and manifest our desire. In this regard, we must be encouraged to use techniques we find personally satisfying. That is, the techniques themselves help catalyze our passion. We have to take ownership of all we do. Otherwise we are giving away our power to another. Anything we use, including thoughts and ideas that we don't make our own, causes us to give away some of our creative power and creative ability. We have to take ownership of what we give away.

I learned to set my intentions on a daily basis and soon it became a natural thing to do, a success habit. It's something that you can do that will speed up your success cycle. What is it you want to experience for that day? Do you want to connect with people? Do you want to have the best day? Do you want to feel accomplished? Just set that intention and put it out there. For some reason, the universe will provide; it will open the gates and allow you to achieve whatever you intended to achieve.

▶ | **Questions**

1. Why is it important to set intensions?

2. Have you ever professed an intention and it came to a reality without much effort?

3. What do you want to experience tomorrow?

_____

_____

_____

_____

_____

_____

_____

_____

_____

This is an Interactive Book with Free Videos!

Please register by visiting the website, and get instant access to **17 FREE videos** that summarize each chapter. Simply go to:

www.MidasMindsetBook.com

or scan this QR code with your smartphone.

▶ | Notes

_____

_____

_____

_____

▶ | 4

Daily Success Habits

Your Net Worth is usually determined by what remains after your bad habits are subtracted from your good habits…

—Benjamin Franklin

There is a myth about the overnight success, a lot of people think that it comes easily one random day. Achievers wake up one day and all of a sudden they're successful—but that's not how it works. Actually, that's far from how it works. There are no overnight sensations. There is no overnight success. If you see somebody who is successful, most likely it is someone who has worked hard, setting their goals and intentions, and went about getting what he or she wanted. For example, when Manny Pacquiao beat Oscar De La Hoya the first time, nobody knew about this new boxing champion. He went in the boxing ring and out-boxed Oscar De La Hoya for many rounds. Now, do you think that he just woke up that day and decided to just go into the ring and beat up Oscar De La Hoya and take his title? Absolutely not. Manny Pacquiao had been training for a lifetime. Waking up at 5:00 in the morning, eating healthy food, doing all the exercises, being away from his family and training hard most of his life to get this chance to shine. He earned the right to be in that situation. He took full advantage of the opportunity to be the better fighter that night. That's how success works. It's a daily occurrence of small wins, small victories. Nobody wakes up successful; that just doesn't exist. It's a major misconception in society I like to look at success as something that should be done on a daily basis. Success is a habit. If we wake up early and we have a successful day early on, we just accelerate our success. Sometimes we wake up early and we don't necessarily have a successful morning. The good news is it's not how you start, but it's how you finish. End up finishing that day on a successful note and improve in small increments , the next day. Success is a daily habit. You can just wake up one day and say, "Okay. I'm going to be successful today," and be successful. But to do that, you have to have successful habits.

Take a look at how your day starts. Were you organized enough to know where your day was going? Did you put your intentions out there? A key factor in achieving success is to utilize your time and make the most of each hour. Some people who have succeeded believe it is due to the long hours they work. They get up early, focus on their day, and prepare to challenge anything that comes along. Ask yourself what is necessary to do today to achieve your intended goal. Write down your tasks then say them out loud. By doing this you are setting your intentions.

We all have the potential to succeed. Success is not something only a few can have. Success can happen to anyone at any time, all it takes is the desire, because we all have the potential. We also have the capability of failing as well. By telling yourself daily that you *can't* do something, you can't find a job, you can't finish writing your book, you can't…you fill in the blanks. These beliefs are called "false beliefs" and they limit you from reaching your full potential.

This gets us back to our *intentions*. Instead of telling yourself what you *can't* do, tell the universe what you *can* do, what you will do. Get rid of all those false beliefs and get the success you deserve. Don't sit around and think of all the reasons that these bad things have happened to you. Think of yourself as being in charge, you are the master of your thoughts. Instead of focusing on the external reasons, focus on the internal, and change your way of thinking.

You can jump start your new habits 5 minutes at a time. When I wanted be a better reader, I started reading 5 minutes at a time. When I wanted to get in shape, I would exercise for only 5 minutes. When I wanted to learn how to meditate, I would lay down at the beach for

5 minutes only. These 5 minutes seemed like an eternity. But after repetition these 5 minutes became 15, then 30 minutes plus. This works for many things. I must warn you, will power is usually non-sustainable. If you want to completely integrate anything, you must make it part of your identity. The next chapter we'll dive deeper into your personal identity. This is one of the most powerful things you can learn.

▶ | Questions

1. Success is something that occurs over night. True or False

2. To change a habit, how many minutes should you start with?

3. Will power usually wears off, what should you do to integrate the change you want?

_____

_____

_____

_____

_____

_____

_____

_____

_____

This is an Interactive Book with Free Videos!

Please register by visiting the website, and get instant access to **17 FREE videos** that summarize each chapter. Simply go to:

www.MidasMindsetBook.com

or scan this QR code with your smartphone.

▶ | **Notes**

▶ | 5

Fail Forward toward Success

It is impossible to live without failing at something, unless you live so cautiously that you might as well not have lived at all, in which case you have failed by default.

—J. K. Rowling

Failure is the price of admission in order to succeed. Any highly successful person would agree. So why are we taught from the time we are young, and throughout our life, not to fail? Society tells us this is one of the most important things we can do in life. To be safe, we are told to plan ahead, put our ducks in a row, and succeed. It becomes fearful for us to fail. In general, the majority of the planet is scared to fail and to look foolish amongst friends, family, spouses and co-workers. When we're scared to fail, we don't even try. We become paralyzed and more often than not, we expire and take the gift that God gifted us to the grave. This to me is the definition of failure. To not explore and expand on the one this special gift that would fulfill us and give our lives a sense of accomplishment

There have been many studies done on young people showing how successful they have become. So, why are these people successful while others aren't? Because they have more confidence and they try new things more often, which is really one of the biggest things that separate the so-called successful people from those people who are less successful. The fact is, some people explore more possibilities and experiences. This allows them to find new avenues of joy and in the process a sense of happiness and self-discovery. According to Abraham Lincoln, Success is going from failure to failure without losing enthusiasm.

In order for you to succeed, you have to be able to accept and embrace failure. You're going to fail a whole lot more than you will succeed, especially when you are first starting out. It's important to pivot if necessary. If you ask anybody who is highly successful, they're going to tell you the same. They're going to tell you the only reason they're successful is because they're willing to fail and they're not scared to fail. There is no success without failure. This is one of

As long as you learn from your own mistakes, there is no such thing as failure. Let failure be your teacher, not your enemy. You must embrace this new ideology of failing as not a failure, but as a learning experience. Embrace it like a sign that you are on the right track, and just change the way you perceive failure and the way you react to it. It would be great if we could all succeed the first time we try something, but trial and error appears to be the process here. As soon as you see the failure coming on, don't let your ego take over, instead put your defense mechanisms aside. We may think that to save face we need to quit and find something else to do. But that is exactly what we don't want to do; even if that is a natural reaction to our difficult task.

Learn from Your Failures

We all know that persistence pays off in the end. We've heard it all our lives and are often told that a failed project is considered failure. But is it really? Go back to that project.. take another look. You've attempted something that you know will work because it's your idea and you've worked hard to see it to fruition. So, now that you've recognized your failure, you should be able to take your project and pivot with the feedback you have leaned from the experience. Ask for feedback from those who have walked that path, get advice from people who have experience and have failed also. This can be some of the best guidance you will ever receive. If you think no one wants to help you, you are mistaken. Most of us love to see other take action in the right direction and we love to assist in your entrepreneurial journey. Don't let your ego get in the way; Ask for help because you can't do it alone. Some people have advice that may move the project forward and save you a small fortune from their experience. Now from my own experience, the bigger I fail, the bigger the lessons. I learn a little bit from my successes, but so much more from my failures. The more expensive the lesson is, the more I internalize it. Some mistakes I only make once because they are so painful that I never want to repeat them again. Fail forward, fail fast, fail small, and change your mind about failing. This alone will improve your success rate tremendously.

► | **Questions**

1. True or False : Failure is part of the success process.

2. Why should you ask others with experience for advice, insight or guidance?

3 . Do you know anyone who failed and adjusted strategies and had a great outcome?

_____

_____

_____

_____

_____

_____

_____

_____

_____

This is an Interactive Book with Free Videos!

Please register by visiting the website, and get instant access to **17 FREE videos** that summarize each chapter. Simply go to:

www.MidasMindsetBook.com

or scan this QR code with your smartphone.

▶ | **Notes**

▶ | 6

Progress vs. Perfection

Perfection is not attainable, but if we chase perfection we can catch excellence.

—Vince Lombardi

This one is so difficult for me because I have been a perfectionist for most of my life. That has hindered my success in a variety of ways. I don't know where it comes from but this is one of the things I still battle. I'm still challenged by it but I'm getting so much better.

Progress is so much more impactful than perfection. Let me give you an example. Writing this book is the perfect example. *Midas Mindset for Gentepreneurs* is my first published book. It is far from perfect. As a matter of fact, a year from now I will probably look back and be embarrassed. I have to constantly remind myself that it's my first and I shouldn't expect a masterpiece. At times, my personal standards are very high and I often fall short. My second book will be better. Hopefully one day I will write my 8th book and look at it and be content. So what keeps me moving forward? The principles in this book have changed my life. If I share them with you, there is a chance that it can help you rediscover and improve the quality of your life. I would hate to rob you from this experience because of my insecurities of being an Author.

I don't consider myself a writer, but my purpose is to bring you value and this is one of the platforms that I can relate to because I have read books that have helped me along with my personal journey. There is no value in me hording my gift because of my personal insecurities. I would like you to keep in mind, I'm just like you. Nothing about me is superior. I've spent time developing my Midas Mindset and so can you.

Another example: When I first started filming content videos and many know I'm big on video marketing—it was early 2008, 2009. For years and years I recorded videos, sometimes recording one video so many times that I would just stop and never edit or post them. Right before I started Gentepreneur.com I said to myself, "Look, for the next month you're going to record one video each week and you're going to do it with one take. It doesn't matter how good or how bad it is. You are going to post it without editing it and you're going to post it online, and then you're going to post it on Facebook.

I remember the first video I recorded. I recorded it at one of my businesses that I was closing. I just did a one shot, one kill, and I posted it, and I remember how painful it felt to push that send button. It was almost like a physical pain but I did it anyways. Then the next week I recorded another video without editing. It was also far from perfect but I sent it out, and it was still just as painful as the first one. Then I recorded another video at the beach. I recorded it and I posted it and it was even more painful because I truly didn't like this video.

Guess what? The pain is sometimes still there. But now I just let it go. Not perfect, no problem. We're imperfect beings. That perfection stopped my growth for so many years. It's hard when you try to reach perfection with everything you do. But overcame that. Now I'm imperfect and things have become so much easier. I'm just a regular person, and people connect with me more when I'm imperfect. Don't be afraid to make mistakes. By expecting perfection in ourselves or others, co-workers of those we love, we are setting ourselves up for disappointment. A person who strives for perfection above all else is often going to be disappointed, and disappointment itself causes us grief, and often alienates us from those closest to it.

There is nothing wrong with striving for perfection. We all want to do our best. But when our goal isn't reached and our standards are lowered, all kinds of disorders can take place, especially for those who are completely driven by perfection. Being driven by perfection can often become an addiction in itself. In our culture we are constantly being bombarded with suggestions putting an emphasis on being perfect. We make sure our children have good, if not perfect, grades. We tend to measure our lives in terms of success and failure. In other words, we often forget the true meaning of life and any sense of balance we have.

By striving for perfection in an unhealthy way, we often forget about our environment and our part in it. Being perfect is a state of mind—your mind. However, if someone ever did fulfill this state of absolute perfection, chances are the extreme perfectionist would not be good company for others. The perfectionist, however, wouldn't be able to tolerate the imperfections of others and most likely unable enjoy the company of those people who have not been driven by perfection.

By always valuing our performance over serenity, no matter what we are doing, we sacrifice our ability to be in balance, our core values. To have a full life, we need the harmonization of peace of mind, health, and happiness. Excellence is a better bench mark to strive for … With a lot of practice you will eventually reach a level of mastery.

▶ | **Questions**

1. Perfection is the enemy of progress: True of False

2. Have you ever procrastinated or failed to do finish something because it wasn't perfect?

3. Describe a time were you did your best and it was far from perfect but it was more than enough.

_____

_____

_____

_____

_____

_____

_____

_____

This is an Interactive Book with Free Videos!

Please register by visiting the website, and get instant access to **17 FREE videos** that summarize each chapter. Simply go to:

www.MidasMindsetBook.com

or scan this QR code with your smartphone.

▶ | Notes

_____

_____

_____

_____

Marcos Orozco

► | 7

Making Decisions with Core Values

When your values are clear to you, making decisions becomes easier.

—Roy E. Disney

What are core values? Core values are the guiding principles that dictate your actions and behaviors. Where do your core values come from? Most come at an early age from family, teachers, people of influence and environment. Values are often the compass that helps you choose between behaviors and actions. Values help you decide your priorities in business and personal life. When friends ask me for advice, I often tell them to follow their hearts and make the right decision every chance they get. The "right" decision often depends on their values. Let me give you an example. Let's pretend you are playing with your young son or daughter and you both find a brown leather wallet full of crispy $100 bills. The way you handle this situation has everything to do with your values. You have many options but two are obvious. You could keep the money and wallet or you can contact the owner via address on the license. If you value honesty and being a great role model for your child, the decision is quite easy. Not all examples are black and white. This is where things become more difficult and we tend to put decisions on hold.. If you procrastinate on decisions, that is a recipe for pain especially in the business world. People who are highly successful make decisions quick. Whether it's a wrong decision or the right decision, they make a decision. Why is this important? Because you have to pick a side whether in a personal of business environment. On the freeway you either go right or left or else you will crash into the center divider. You have to make a decision about things to keep moving forward. If it's the wrong decision, the quicker you find out it's a wrong decision the quicker you can pivot and adjust. If you make a decision and it's the right decision, awesome. You keep going. You're going to move forward a lot faster. And if it's not the correct decision, you can always try again.

Values can change from time to time. Before my son Noah was born, I would often hang out with friends on the weekends till sunrise. Now that I'm a father, my values have drastically changed for the better. I now chose to spend my time with my son. I make it a mission to make that time 'quality time' for both of us. I want to give him a great experience and create bonding memories. Odds are when he's an adult; I will alter my values once again. There are many resources online for exercises that help you find your core values.

▶ | **Questions**

1. What are core values

2. Where do core values come from?

3. Write down the top 3 core values for you?

This is an Interactive Book with Free Videos!

Please register by visiting the website, and get instant access to **17 FREE videos** that summarize each chapter. Simply go to:

www.MidasMindsetBook.com

or scan this QR code with your smartphone.

▶ | Notes

_____

_____

_____

_____

▶ | 8

Leadership Starts with You

Men make history and not the other way around. In periods where there is no leadership, society stands still. Progress occurs when courageous, skillful leaders seize the opportunity to change things for the better.

—Harry Truman

Leadership is often confused with management. These are different disciplines. Not all leaders are great managers and vice versa. Leaders lead by example and often make the money in the market place. Aside from the money, it is important to improve on these skill sets because people are hungry for guidance and reassurance. From families to corporate and business environments, leaders are often the beacons of light in dark and uncertain times. At times, I consider myself a good leader, but I strive to be better each day and one day I hope to achieve my best so I can demonstrate to my son what is possible.

You too can become a great leader by practice and learning from the greats. All great leaders are visionaries with the ability to inspire others to work towards their unified vision. When I think about great visionaries, I think Steve Jobs, Richard Branson and Ion Musk to name a few. Their view of the world is very different than most of ours. Without free thinkers and visionaries, we wouldn't have airplanes, automobiles or even spaceships. We wouldn't have cell phones or even computers. Studies show leadership positions pay much more in the corporate world. In family settings, the head of the family in a leadership role can be the glue to keep the family together during troubling times. I believe leaders are made not born. Whether you are leading you family or employees, you must possess specific qualities to succeed. Can you have natural tendencies to be a leader, yes; but this alone is not enough to be an effective leader. This is a skill that takes years, if not decades, to hone.

There are many qualities and skills you must refine to lead others to the Promised Land. These are just a couple of examples of some of the skills it takes to become great. Honesty is critical. In times of uncertainty, you must be able to look at your people and give them a clear understanding of the situation, even if it's difficult. The ability to make difficult decisions comes with the territory. You can't hesitate or show weakness because you may lose credibility with your emotions of doubt.

How you communicate is critical and a skill that pays off exponentially. Effective communication is monumental for any leadership role. You don't have to be charismatic, but you do have to be confident. From my personal experience, the most difficult skill for me to learn was proper delegation. This is where good management comes in. And the most important quality as far as I'm concerned is staying focused and having a clear vision of the big picture for both your family and your business endeavors.

▶ | Questions

1. Leaders often make more money in the market place: True of false

2. Have you worked for a good leader? What made that person effective?

3. What is one thing you can do to improve your leadership skills.

This is an Interactive Book with Free Videos!

Please register by visiting the website, and get instant access to **17 FREE videos** that summarize each chapter. Simply go to:

www.MidasMindsetBook.com

or scan this QR code with your smartphone.

▶ | Notes

▶ | 9

Abundant Mindset

To live a pure unselfish life, one must count nothing as one's own in the midst of abundance.

—Buddha

I heard a story the other day. A gentleman was in a small fishing town and there were two buckets. One of them had a lid on it and the other one didn't. Tourists who wandered by asked the fisherman, "Why is there a lid in that bucket of crabs and the other crab bucket has no lid?"

He said, "Oh, it's because these Asiatic crabs will help each other out. They will get together and they'll collaborate, and soon they will get each other out of that bucket one by one by working together, and they will escape." Then he said, "The other bucket that has no lid on it, those are Latin crabs. Those crabs, when one of the crabs is rising to the top, will pull it down so they never get to escape."

This short story you just read is about having an abundant mindset. There's so much wealth, there's so much abundance in this planet. When somebody is active in success and making money, it doesn't mean they're taking away your share. It signifies that if it's possible for them, it's possible for you. If you feel uncomfortable, it's because you might not be living out to your full potential. There is so much abundance in this world and more than enough for everybody.

When you envy somebody who is being successful, you're only hurting yourself. By telling your subconscious mind that this is wrong, you are actually hating and limiting yourself. You're deactivating your potential by doing that.

Having a mindset of abundance will elevate your success to incredible heights. I've been blessed with this mindset since I was young. Not all the time, though. I'm not perfect, but most of the time I will congratulate people who are doing well. If I see somebody doing better than me I say, "Awesome, man. Good job." That means if he's doing it, I can learn to do it too. With every business I had, I would teach my employees that showed interest everything I knew. Why? You might ask, because I believe and I live in abundance. I know that there's more than enough to go around. Guess what? If they're going to leave my company and they're going to go out and do their own thing, I bless them. I'm not afraid of that. I never had an employee leave me to branch out on his or her own. If that happened I would wish him the best. I'm here to serve. I'm here to help. Abundance is something that will take your success to new levels and abundance is something that can be shared.

What do you do when you have an abundance of something; let's say vegetables from your garden, money or knowledge. You share! That's how abundance works. And by doing so, you are also helping to improve your own life in many ways. By sharing your abundance, you are bringing joy to your life. Remember the saying, "Pay it forward?" That's what is happening. And it doesn't necessarily mean monetary help. There are all kinds of ways to help someone. Find out what they need most and give with no strings attached.

▶ | Questions

1. Having a mindset of abundance will elevate your success to incredible heights. True or False

2. Describe one time that you felt uncomfortable because your were envy of someone else's success.

3. Have you delivered good news to someone and they reacted different than you imagined, if so, how did that make you feel?

_____

_____

_____

_____

_____

_____

_____

_____

This is an Interactive Book with Free Videos!

Please register by visiting the website, and get instant access to **17 FREE videos** that summarize each chapter. Simply go to:

www.MidasMindsetBook.com

or scan this QR code with your smartphone.

▶ | Notes

_____

_____

_____

_____

Midas Mindset for Genteprenuers

▶ | 10

How to Manifest Your Thoughts into Reality

Never let life impede on your ability to manifest your dreams. Dig deeper into your dreams and deeper into yourself and believe that anything is possible, and make it happen.

—Corin Nemec

You and I manifest our thoughts into reality all the time. Let's talk about manifestation. How do we manifest things? I have something I created called the V.I.D.E.O.

technique; it's an acronym for Visualize it Daily and Emotionalize the Outcome, VIDEO.

Manifesting is reaching out to God or the universe with what you desire. For instance, you wake up in the morning and before you get out of bed, or even after, take a moment to think about what you are trying to achieve. Keep it up throughout the day. We are asking the universe for guidance to achieve what it is we want to do with our life right now.

Some people refer to *The Universe* as God or a supreme being. It is the life force that surrounds us, it is energy and comprised of everything. All of this follows the Law of Attraction; what we 'manifest' we can achieve, we attract to us what we desire. If you stop and think about it, we have been opening our minds to this concept all along; through our thoughts. Our thoughts have energy, and energy flows, and through this communication, and through our thoughts, we allow the universe to deliver.

This is how this came about for me. When I was younger I played baseball. I was really, really good at it. I stopped playing after high school, but decided to play again at the age of 35. I played for an adult league. When I decided to go back to playing baseball, man, I was on fire! I went 13 for 13 for the first three games and I was hot. I was hitting that ball hard.

Of course this hitting statistic was unsustainable, but I was still a really solid baseball hitter. Some guys who used to play high-caliber baseball in a professional level would come up to me and ask, "Why is it that you hit so well when you haven't played for such a long time?"

I didn't know how to answer them, until the night before playing in a playoff game. When I closed my eyes before going to sleep, I started visualizing myself hitting that ball hard. I can see it right now as I'm writing about it. That ball came towards me fast, but I could see the laces. I could just take a swing at it and POW; I would hit and drive it so hard I could feel it. I would emotionalize that and feel strong, visualizing myself as a strong baseball player. I would do this again and again until I feel asleep. Then first thing in the morning I would start to visualize this scenario again and again. So when it was time for me to play baseball, I was a great hitter. This interesting thing about your imagination is that your subconscious mind doesn't know you're pretending. It believes that it is a real live event. Then it creates or carves new neurological pathways in your brain.

I remember hearing a story once about a runner who said he would visualize himself winning the race. He said that it always gave him an edge against the other runners. I realized that if you visualize yourself doing something and doing it well, and visualize it over and over again and emotionalize the outcome, you will manifest whatever it is that you're visualizing.

I began to do this over and over and over again in my head. When I awoke before the game I would send these thoughts out to the universe again and again, visualizing myself hitting that ball hard. No matter what your walk of life, you CAN manifest and attract to you what you want.

Sometimes writers visualize their novel getting picked up by an agent and even visualize signing a contract for a book deal. They continue to put this out there, knowing this is their goal, this is what they are working toward, and believing in the laws of the universe.

Some people even stick a picture or a visual image to their refrigerator that shows them hitting the ball, signing the contract, running the race, etc. There are even people who have found their mate or future spouse through manifestation. Visualize you are with the person you want to be with, the kind of person who makes you happy and has common interests. But don't dwell on it, put it out there and let it simmer. But believe. Because if you are wary of this happening, odds are it may not happen. Odds are you have also manifested things without much effort. The most common visualizations are for cars or houses. We get what we focus on most of the time. If this is the case, then focus on what you want in life. Focus on the good things and not the bad.

This is how you manifest your dreams and goals. You visualize it. One of the first things I ever manifested was a vehicle that I wanted when I was young. I couldn't stop thinking about it. I thought about how it would feel when I drove the vehicle. I even thought about the color paint it had and the type of wheels it had. The more details in your imagination the better. Guess what? I was able to buy that vehicle. I made it look the way I wanted it to look. I manifested that car.

Technically we are always manifesting. Each thought we send out allows energy to flow to that desire; which may be good advice when people say. "Be careful what you wish for." You don't want to manifest what could potentially hurt you. Our thoughts create who we are. Some say we ask for everything we get in our life through our thoughts, and as long as we don't block our beliefs, intentions, or flow of energy, we can manifest greatness. Once you recognize the negative thoughts that keep you from realizing your dreams, clear those blocks. Clean up those thoughts and let those positive manifestations occur.

So, how do we do that? First of all, begin by asking the universe to free you from the negativity and thoughts that are blocking the flow. Reach out to the universe daily, or more often, and pray to let go of your limited beliefs.

What we dream, we attract; whether it be love, health, or whatever.

Stay Committed to the Goal

What is your primary goal? Is it to be happy? By internalizing happiness, you are bound to reflect that happiness, and yes, attract it to you. If you are going through bad times, experiencing something in your life that is harming you, it's a good time to take a deep breath and blow out all that negativity. By thinking about it and filling our thoughts with it, guess what? We are attracting it.

If you think about it, you have got to believe it. There are all kinds of ways to make your intentions known. Spend some time sitting with your desire, think about it, and let it wash over you. Meditation is a great way to put your desires out there, and visualizing is another. Whatever it is that puts you in that place of letting your feelings get in touch with your energy. If you believe it, it is there. Contemplate, believe and feel.

Now that you've put your intentions out there, it's time to wait. Wait and trust that the universe has a plan for you. You're not able to put a time frame on manifesting so just relax and trust. By diligently practicing and cleaning out the negative flow, you are on your way to manifesting what you desire.

▶ | **Questions**

1. What does V.I.D.E.O. stand for?

2. What is one thing that you couldn't stop thinking about and you manifested?

_____

_____

_____

_____

_____

_____

This is an Interactive Book with Free Videos!

Please register by visiting the website, and get instant access to **17 FREE videos** that summarize each chapter. Simply go to:

www.MidasMindsetBook.com

or scan this QR code with your smartphone.

▶ | Notes

_____

_____

_____

_____

▶ | 11

Stop Judging People

Our prime purpose in this life is to help others.
And if you can't help them, at least don't hurt them.

—Dalai Lama

Judging people is a hidden habit that keeps us from achieving higher levels of success. Passing judgment on others isn't good for anybody. Not good for yourself, not good for the person you're judging; in fact it is more harmful to you than the person you are judging. By judging others, maybe subconsciously you are judging yourself. When you look at somebody and have ill thoughts against that person, your subconscious mind thinks it's looking in the mirror and it's judging itself. This is counterproductive. You are working to change your identity but at the same time you're judging people? This is a conflict that needs to be overcome if you are to change the way you think and look at yourself and others. To your subconscious mind, this is conflict. The best way to stop judging people is to become aware each time you do it. Instead of judging that person, give him or her a blessing, find something good about them. Drop the ego. We are all imperfect and we are doing the best we can.

For instance, when you see a homeless person, you may think, "Poor guy. I feel bad for that person." It's better to change that thought. Instead say, "That gentleman has infinite potential, and I hope one day he can use that potential and become the best he can be." Wish him well. It's very powerful. Judgment is something that hinders our growth dramatically. I didn't know I was a judgmental person until I became aware that I was judging others. I never thought of myself as a judgmental person because I'm a nice guy, and I never thought I'd have ill thoughts against people.

I didn't always have ill thoughts, but I did catch myself judging people subconsciously, and especially homeless people. Not in a bad way, but I used to say, or think, "Man, poor guy. I feel bad for him." That gentleman has infinite potential, and I hope one day he excels in what he wants to do in life." Instead of feeling sorry for someone you think is bad off, give him a mental blessing. It's an empowering feeling for both people. Even though he can't hear you, your thoughts are energy, and they are flowing and empowering the person.

Let's face it, we all judge people or things at one time or another. But if we stop and recognize what we are doing and are mindful of others and their feelings, we can stop. Let's say we are judgmental against people who smoke, or eat too much junk food and are destroying their health. It is an automatic response for most of us to think badly about the way the person is treating his or her body. We think of all the health issues associated with it and get frustrated that there is nothing we can do about it.

Before you judge that person, think about what he or she may be going through. We don't know. Maybe this person is depressed and chooses food or cigarettes to make her feel better. We don't know what has happened in their lives and we don't know what they've been through. By putting your focus on judging that person—who may be a friend, a relative, or even someone we don't know—we are saying that we don't appreciate that person. Our focus is in the wrong place. Instead think about the person as someone with good qualities, someone who brings much into the world.

By judging the individual, we are not only hurting them, we are also hurting ourselves by becoming frustrated and unhappy about not being able to do something about it. And who are we to judge anyhow?

How Can We Overcome Being Judgmental?

The first thing we can do is being aware of what we are doing. When you see this happening, stop yourself. If you find yourself becoming angry and frustrated at the individual, stop, recognize that you are being judgmental, and move on. It's not that you are being a bad person with your judgment, but you have learned this behavior and now it's time to change it, or at least recognize it.

Ask yourself what you are being judgmental about? Is it important? Do you have such high expectations of this person that it's necessary for you to feel this way? What are some of the things that you like about that person? Let the 'likes' overpower the dislikes. Put yourself in their shoes.

Now that you can recognize when you are being judgmental, you can ask yourself what you can do for that person. Is there anything you can do to lighten the load that person is going through?

Turn your judgment into curiosity and empathy and you'll both be a lot happier for it. Look for the good in people instead of their flaws. This will help you on your own personal growth in a tremendous way.

▶ | **Questions**

1. When you judge someone you are really judging yourself: True or false

2. Describe a time when someone judged you and he or she was wrong about you.

_____

_____

_____

_____

_____

_____

_____

_____

_____

This is an Interactive Book with Free Videos!

Please register by visiting the website, and get instant access to **17 FREE videos** that summarize each chapter. Simply go to:

www.MidasMindsetBook.com

or scan this QR code with your smartphone.

▶ | Notes

_____

_____

_____

_____

▶ | 12

Balance Is for Circus Animals

A balanced life is like a bland soup. . .pass me the pepper

—Marcos Orozco

Balance is great for circus performances. This idea of living a balanced life is cliché to me. I might offend some people but hear me out on this one. Let's talk about balancing your family, health, spirituality and your career to name a few. First of all, it's impossible to balance and if it were possible, it would be minimal return on your happiness. I believe our main focus should be on experiences that create joy in our lives. After this, you can try to be balanced in other areas of your life. My number one joy is spending time with my son. Everything else is secondary. A close second is my personal journey, my purpose and creating value for my fellow Gentepreneurs. Following my bliss. Funny thing is both of these almost seem one in the same. This will change as he gets older and lives a life on his own as an adult. This is why there could never be true balance, because we are constantly evolving.

We should strive for more of an adaptive balance; always adjusting the sails to your boat or better yet, switching gears on a bicycle. Life is similar to riding a bicycle, balance is necessary but without movement, balance doesn't matter much. You have to consider many other things when riding a bicycle. How fast should you peddle, you have to be aware of your surrounding for safety, follow traffic laws; and all while trying to enjoy your time. Sure, balance is important. For me, having the cool wind blowing past me, and watching the sunset at the beach is my main focus. The balance somewhat happens automatically, like magic. Most of us beat ourselves up so much trying to be balanced. In conclusion, don't be so harsh, enjoy the bicycle ride.

▶ | Questions

1. Having an unbalanced life is unrealistic: True or False

2. Life is short, you should enjoy with experiences as much as you possibly can: True of false

3. What is the one thing that brings joy into your heart?

_____

_____

_____

_____

_____

_____

_____

This is an Interactive Book with Free Videos!

Please register by visiting the website, and get instant access to **17 FREE videos** that summarize each chapter. Simply go to:

www.MidasMindsetBook.com

or scan this QR code with your smartphone.

▶ | Notes

_____

_____

_____

Midas Mindset for Gentreprenuers

▶ | 13

Two Types of Motivation

A creative man is motivated by the desire to achieve, not by the desire to beat others.

—Ayn Rand

Let's talk about motivation. What motivates us? There are several different ways that we become motivated. We're either motivated towards a result or away from a consequence. This has been one of the biggest challenges for some of my successes and failures. It's the yo-yo effect. Let me give you an example of how I changed my thoughts and my motivation.

When I was younger, I used to tell myself I didn't want to be broke anymore and that motivated me. To keep me from being broke, I worked hard so I would be comfortable. But since I wasn't broke anymore, my motivation disappeared. Eventually through self-sabotage, I went back to being broke. This happens a lot with diets where people have these inner thoughts about losing weight and being thin, so they get into a healthy lifestyle.

They start eating healthy, they exercise or starve themselves, and all of a sudden, they're not "fat." But before you know it, they lose that motivation and go back to their old ways, eventually becoming overweight once again. That's why they call it 'yo-yo dieting'.

There's a simple solution to keeping your success though. For example, every time I wake in the morning, I don't say to myself, "Why am I working so hard? Because I don't want to be broke." Instead I tell myself the reason I'm waking up early is to start work, which will allow me to have a great life with my son. By being motivated, I can afford to travel with him anywhere and anytime I want. But most important is that I am able to show him what is possible. I want to give him that gift even if I never had that for myself. That's what keeps my motivation going.

So, in the case of losing weight, there are things you can tell yourself to keep you motivated. If I wanted to stay healthy, instead of saying, "I don't want to be fat," I may say "I'm motivated towards a healthier lifestyle." I want to be able to look in the mirror and be happy with what I see. I want to be able to put on clothes and have them fit properly. I want to have abundant energy so I can do anything I want and feel good about it."

Those are just two minor examples, but this has everything to do with the questions you're asking yourself. The better quality question we ask our self, the better quality of life, according to Anthony Robbins. When we ask ourselves a question, we get a response from our brain. If I ask myself, "Why am I stupid?" guess what's going to happen? My brain is going to go find the answer for that. It's going to tell me something like, "Well, you were dropped as a baby," or "You did a lot of drugs when you were younger," or "You drank yourself silly," or "God just made you that way." Now, none of these things are probably true, but if I ask, it's going to answer me. I could turn that around and ask myself a similar question; why am I so smart? The brain's going to come up with an answer.

"Well, because you have read a lot." Or, "You know what, your parents are smart," or, "because you ask inquisitive questions ," Or "You're special," or because you don't watch television.

I don't know for sure. I've never really asked myself those questions; these are just examples. Keep in mind, there's a conversation going on in your head. If we break down the conversation, it's your brain sharing information from your point of view, or your experiences.

Take a look at our thoughts for instance.

If our thoughts motivate us, then we have to monitor the deliberations, the dialogue going on inside our heads. Ask better questions. The better the quality of a question you ask yourself, the better our quality of life. To give you an example, let's pretend you're in sales and you're continually getting difficult customers. You may say, "Why is it I always get the customers who don't buy?"

Now, that question is loaded to work against you; because remember, what you ask will get an answer. A better question would be, "How can I provide more value for my customers to get them to purchase items and continue to shop here?" That's a much better question. You will get the answer according to how you ask it.

Let me give you the last example. "Why am I overweight? Why can't I eat healthier? Why can't I stop eating ice cream?" Or, you could say, "How can I make better choices when I eat so I can be fit?" Or, "What type of fruits and vegetables should I eat so I can have more energy?"

It's simply a matter of rephrasing the questions and this takes a little bit of practice, but just like anything else, the more you practice, the better you get at it. This will give you an immediate return on your investment. The better quality questions, the better quality of life.

This is an Interactive Book with Free Videos!

Please register by visiting the website, and get instant access to **17 FREE videos** that summarize each chapter. Simply go to:

www.MidasMindsetBook.com

or scan this QR code with your smartphone.

▶ | **Notes**

_____

_____

_____

_____

Midas Mindset for Genteprenuers

▶ | 14

Identity Yourself

> *In the social jungle of human existence, there is no feeling of being alive without a sense of identity.*
>
> —Erik Erikson

How we see ourselves is more important than how others see us. The story we tell ourselves is the story we grow into. Let me share with you a personal experience I had a long time ago. My first professional job was selling cars at South Bay Jeep in Torrance, California. I learned how to sell cars, but my success felt limited and my paycheck reflected that limitation. The issue was I saw myself as a young adult with a colorful history that happens to be selling cars. Only until I changed the way I saw myself did I start making a huge contribution to the company and my paycheck was looking much better. I started to identify myself as a entrepreneur that happens to be working at this car dealer. My perception of myself changed along with the story I replayed over and over in my head. My demeanor, attitude and even the way I walked was altered unconsciously without much effort. This gave me confidence to learn new skill sets and tools to eventually open a couple of successful ventures later in my career.

Another example that comes to mind is a story about me smoking cigarettes like a chimney. Long time ago, when I was younger, I used to drink a lot, I used to use drugs, and I used to smoke cigarettes. Eventually I stopped drinking and abusing drugs, but I was still smoking cigarettes. I remember while driving one time and listening to the radio the host of that show said, "If you want to stop smoking cigarettes, this is how you do it. This is the magic formula, the magic potion, the secret sauce." The man in from the radio program continued to say "You have to identify yourself as a nonsmoker."

He went on to explain that how you see yourself is how you act on a subconscious level. So, if you were to start looking in the mirror and saying, "You know what? I'm a nonsmoker. I choose not to smoke. I could smoke, but I choose not to," you are putting out your intentions. You are telling yourself and the universe that you are a non-smoker. Instead of saying, "I can't smoke," tell yourself that you *choose* not to smoke. Take a look in the mirror and identify yourself as a nonsmoker. I started visualizing how a non-smoker felt when he goes for a run? How do his clothes smell after a long day at the office? How is his oral hygiene? I started doing that. I started changing the way I saw myself as a smoker, and guess what? Well, without effort I stopped smoking. I don't even know how, I don't even know when, but I do know that I stopped smoking.

This Is How You Change Your Identity

Now, fast forward. We have a lot of identity issues, and we subconsciously begin to act the way we see ourselves. With that being said, if you want to change your identity, there are several things you can do, one of which is writing down how you want to see yourself, how you want to become the best person you can be. Once again, it's that intention.

Write down in specific details what it is you want. Read your list three times a day, morning, afternoon, and again at night for about three weeks. If you want to go longer, even better, but do it at least three times a day for three weeks and see what happens. This is my challenge to you and I would love for you to share your experience with me.

You're going to notice that your identity is going to become, subconsciously, a part of this program. You're going to program your subconscious mind to act like you—how you want to identify yourself. By putting your intentions out there, by *choosing* to be the way you want to be and the person you want others to see you, you can actually change your identity. As you repeat the words, letting out your intentions, your subconscious mind is hearing this. This is one of the easiest ways to change your identity.

So, take a few moments occasionally to really look at who you are at that moment. Is it who you want to be? Is this your true identity? If you are being honest with yourself, you will realize this is not the identity you want, or want others to see. The late Jim Rohn, the legendary personal development guru said, "Success is not a doing process, it is a becoming process. What you do, what you pursue, will elude you—it can be like chasing butterflies. Success is something you attract by the person you become."

In other words; act and behave the way you want to be. If your actions are not what you really want, you will most likely revert back to your old habits. Think and do, but let your mind direct the outcome of your life. Remember—intentions.

▶ | **Questions**

1. How others see you is more important than how you see yourself. True or False

2. Have you ever identified the story you keep telling yourself?

3. What is the easiest way to change your identify?

This is an Interactive Book with Free Videos!

Please register by visiting the website, and get instant access to **17 FREE videos** that summarize each chapter. Simply go to:

www.MidasMindsetBook.com

or scan this QR code with your smartphone.

▶ | **Notes**

Identity Declaration (Write down the perfect you—the person you want to be) Then read this 3 times a day for 3 weeks and see if anything different has happened in your life.

_____

_____

_____

_____

_____

_____

_____

_____

_____

▶ | 15

Invest in Yourself

Invest in the human soul.
Who knows, it might be a diamond in the rough.

—Mary McLeod Bethune

In 2008 the financial collapse took its toll on many industries, including mine. Luckily for me I was acquiring gold and investing in other precious metals. I had multiple investments go south during this time. I was also going to be a first time father. So I had to re-invent myself. During this period in my life, I was voluntarily or involuntarily trading my gold for Knowledge or life lessons. This is where the term Midas Mindset comes from. Looking back, this was a period of tough personal growth. In the previous chapter, I talked about the five things that changed my life. Believe it or not, that was a small investment for the payoff I received in return. So what better than to invest in yourself?

If the best investment is in yourself, then being a passive investor in this area will get you zero results. You must engage and you will notice the benefits rather quickly, in how you think, and how you feel. Most people don't realize that in the journey of so-called success, it's not the things that we acquire, but the person we become. This to me is an incredible advantage to living a life of pure happiness and financial security. When you invest in yourself, that investment never loses value. As a matter of fact, it always gives back. It never stops giving. Your self-investment pays back on a daily basis and the most important thing is that nobody can take it away from you. Investment in yourself never depreciates and never loses value. You can choose to share this information with your son, your daughter, your wife or husband, your parents, or employees, and it can multiply exponentially.

If you don't have much money to investment in yourself, a great place to start is by reading books; books that interest you. Read books about positive mindset and books about your industry. It's always great to read, but for me; it all starts in the mind, to be a positive person and live at the highest conscious level possible. To find inner peace is absolutely priceless. There's no amount of money that can give you inner peace.

Am I saying that money is the root of all evil? No, not at all, it's actually the opposite. Like Les Brown said; the lack of money is the root of all evil. That's where the situation gets difficult for most. When there is no money, people start stealing and robbing and scheming to get money. So find some books that are relevant to your specific needs. Some of the people who write those books will become your mentors. My early book mentors were Dale Carnegie, Zig Ziglar, Brian Tracy, and Jim Rohn.

Before I met Brian Tracy, I had read some of his books. I had heard him speak before and was fortunate enough to meet him. I learned so much from him. Eat Than Frog is one of my favorites. It's about time management. Game changer for me. Another great way to invest in you is to attend events. There are a lot of events in your area that are free for you to attend. Some symposiums will charge a fee. I paid for a seven-day event. $15,000 up front and it was well worth it. Incredible people, great information and I don't regret it one bit. Only once when I implemented what I've learned, did I receive my return on investment.

Mastermind groups are another way to invest in yourself. There you will find like-minded people who want to get ahead in life, people who want to do incredible things and even want to change the world. These are people who are not dreamers, but doers. The power of a mastermind is incredible. So, what is a mastermind group?

When it comes to business, or actually any part of your life, a mastermind group is there to help you with brainstorming, support, and even connecting with the right people you may need to reach your goal as an entrepreneur. It is there to help you achieve success. The great thing about attending groups such as this is that the people in them can challenge each other, acting as devil's advocates, with support. It's a great way to get ideas about things you may not have even thought about, and levering the experience of others, with confidentiality.

Today, we live in an information age where you can go online and learn whatever you want to learn. Just about everything you need to know is online and most of it is free. In this day and age, there are no excuses for not learning new things, new possibilities. It's up to you. Nobody can or will do it for you. One of my favorite quotes is "**Enthusiasm without action is delusion.**" The first time I heard this, I loved it, but with slight discomfort. Because this made me realize I needed to take more action.

Don't forget to apply and take action on the new ideas you learn. Just because you have read numerous books on a subject it doesn't mean you know everything about it. The best way to learn something is by a 'hands on' approach. You could read about swimming for weeks, months, but until you jump in the water and start paddling, it's worthless information. When you pay your gym instructor, he cannot do the sit-ups for you. It doesn't work that way. He can show you how and he can motivate you to get on with it and do some work, but he can't do those exercises for you. If he did, you wouldn't get the results you are trying to achieve. This is what we call *investment*. Your personal investment begins with a decision and only you can make this investment in yourself. It's well worth it. You could pass this on to generations after you. Leave your own legacy. Invest in yourself!

▶ | Questions

1. How much money have you invested in yourself this past 6 months?

2. Have you ever paid someone to be a coach or a mentor?

3. Investing in yourself can never be taken away from you. True or False

_____

_____

_____

_____

_____

_____

_____

_____

This is an Interactive Book with Free Videos!

Please register by visiting the website, and get instant access to **17 FREE videos** that summarize each chapter. Simply go to:

www.MidasMindsetBook.com

or scan this QR code with your smartphone.

▶ | Notes

_____

_____

_____

_____

Midas Mindset for Genteprenuers

▶ | 16

Meditate Vs. Medicate

Spiritual meditation is the pathway to Divinity. It is a mystic ladder which reaches from earth to heaven, from error to truth, from pain to peace.

—James Allen

Nowadays a lot of people are chemically self-medicating, be it with alcohol, heroin, cocaine, marijuana or pharmaceutical drugs. When I was younger I had a host of addictions, to alcohol, to weed, even cocaine, and I experimented with various other drugs. I was doing this to mask emotions that I didn't want to deal with. In so doing was I able to run from my problems.

To get to the next level, to be at peace with myself, the thing that helped me tremendously to overcome such destructive behavior, was meditation. As a Latino, meditation was taboo; almost like witchcraft, what we call *brujería*. My parents especially imposed this belief upon me regarding mediation and other spiritual practices, insisting that yoga and meditation are not appropriate for Christians. I highly disagree.

Meditation is one of the things has taken my personal life, my self-development, to a whole new level. I am very blessed to live a block from the beach and I watch the sunset from the sand every day. In the vein of this tradition, I started meditating for just five minutes at a time. Prior to beginning this practice, there were two specific reasons why I did not meditate. Interestingly enough, one was simply because I did not want to get into a traditional meditation stance or position. I'm not flexible and believed that if I could not place my body in a specific position to meditate then the effort was moot. The second reason was because I had already *tried* to meditate once before and I could not stop my thoughts. I was not aware that such racing thoughts are common when beginning to meditate. One is supposed to allow that happen, and in the unfolding of the meditation, that will eventually stop automatically.

Thoughts will eventually stop appearing during meditation. This is why such a practice is especially valuable to entrepreneurs. The entrepreneurial mind that has a million thoughts running through it, with millions of ideas and a unique tendency to think 10 times ahead of most people. Such a thought process is further encumbered by a condition such as ADHD and a mind that is constantly racing. Imagine a blender left on for 35-years, churning away, placing undue burden on that motor. It is going to burn out eventually.

In meditation, that blender gets unplugged and the motor is allowed to rest. It has made a significant impact on my productivity, enabling me to view things from a different level. It allows me to recoup mental energy. What arises during and after meditation is absolutely incredible. I highly believe that when you pray you talk to God, and when you meditate God talks to you.

If the thought of meditating has ever arisen, do not be afraid to try it for five minutes. There is not right or wrong way to mediate. It is okay to mediate lying down or standing up. It is okay if you do it other ways. It is okay if thoughts keep coming up – there is nothing wrong with that at all. More likely sooner than later, tremendous value will result from meditating, from resting the mind, from unplugging the blender. Problems will be solved at a higher level and things will be seen differently. This is particularly true when under stress; there is no better way to release.

So instead of medicating, meditate.

This is an Interactive Book with Free Videos!

Please register by visiting the website, and get instant access to **17 FREE videos** that summarize each chapter. Simply go to:

www.MidasMindsetBook.com

or scan this QR code with your smartphone.

▶ | 17

My Five Daily Rituals to Success

Successful people are simply those with successful habits.

—Brian Tracy

I want to share with you the beginning of my personal journey, the 5 things that allowed me to discover my purpose and helped me change my life. It happened in a sequence of two mornings, when I noticed there was something wrong in my personal life with my family, my fiancé, and my two-year-old son. Something triggered a sequence of thoughts making me realize that one day I was going to be gone. I was going to leave this earth. I was going to die, and so was his mom. My son is going to have to fend and take care of himself when we are gone. He's going to have to work and be a responsible adult.

I thought about what I could leave him after my death; an estate portfolio, gold or silver, or dare I say a trust fund. Sure, I can leave him tangible things, but 'things' don't always last. Properties can burn down and be destroyed, swindled, or lost in a divorce settlement. His gold could be lost, stolen or even confiscated. So, where does that leave me? That leaves me with what is the most important gift I could leave him—the mindset of infinite possibilities so he can one day follow his own path and take his own personal journey. I don't want him to suffer the way I suffered when I was young. I went through a lot of heartache. I went through depression, alcoholism and drug abuse. Not to mention the difficult financial situations I've been through … I don't want that for him. I wanted better things for him. I don't want him to stumble with all the things I've stumbled with.

That very same day when I thought about it, I made a decision to become the best person I could possibly be and live by example in order to lead my son to be the best possible person he could be. I'm far from perfect, but with only the best of intentions.

I clearly remember walking into our master bedroom early one morning and saying to my fiancé, "Babe, I'm going on a journey, and I want you to come with me, but it's not mandatory. This is something I'm doing for me, for you and for our son. I'm going to get rid of everything I don't like about myself and replace it with great things. I'm going to keep the things that are beneficial and become a better person, the best me. I'm going on this journey starting today!"

My fiancé laughed. "You're crazy," she said. I was so serious that her words didn't register at all, and that was the beginning of my journey.

Have you ever been feed up and wanted to change things or even start all over again? This is exactly what I felt. I decided to become "successful" for the 100th time. This time I was determined to reach a new level. Success is different things to different people, so I didn't know exactly what success was. It could have been monetary, but in reality, I think I was looking for inner peace and happiness.

I went to the computer and Googled "Character traits of successful people." I did some quick research and came up with a simple list of five things; five character traits of successful people. When I did these 5 simple things on a daily basis, I felt within days a shift around me. I feel some new energy that I had never felt before. Keep in mind, things that are simple to do, are also simple not to do.

Try these for 5 things for 5 days and see your life transform.

> **#1 Wake up Early:** Successful people wake up early. Most successful people wake up at 5:00 a.m. So I started waking up early every morning, even if I didn't want to. The early bird catches the worm is what came to mind. It's difficult for me to get up early because my energy level is such that I usually stay up late at night. If you have a habit of

sleeping late and waking up later than you would like, then you are in the right place. The best way to overcome this is to wake up early even if you only slept a couple of hours. After a few long days, this will force your body to sleep earlier. Another thing that helps me sleep earlier and deeper is writing my "to do" list and writing in my journal before I close my eyes to sleep. It helps your subconscious mind to rest, knowing it doesn't have to remind you of these things on your list.

#2 Exercise: The second thing I started doing, which was also the second character trait of highly successful people, was to exercise regularly. Now, at that time in my life I wasn't doing any heavy physical exercise; such as push-ups or lifting weights, etc. I was doing some simple rebounding, which is a fancy word for jumping on the trampoline for 15 minutes a day. It wasn't difficult at all. Even walking for 15 minutes is exercise. Deep breathing exercise is also beneficial to your overall health and very easy to do before you go to sleep. It's so powerful and makes you feel better while your physiology changes and releases natural endorphins. You feel better and have more confidence.

#3 Read: A third character trait that I started doing was reading. It's been said that all successful people read and are 'well read' in an array of subjects. Since all leaders are readers, I began to read on a daily basis. I didn't necessarily consider myself a great reader. To be honest, I still don't consider myself to be a great reader, but I can read a whole lot better than when I started. I started by reading five minutes a day, five little minutes a day, and then I went to six minutes a day. Soon it was seven minutes and then 10 minutes a day, and I started enjoying it, doing 30-60 minutes stretches of reading at a time. Jim Rohn, Les Brown, Brian Tracy, Anthony Robbins and John Maxwell are some of the books I read during this period.

#4 Write: The fourth daily ritual I began doing was to start writing. I kept a journal and wrote about my day, what was going well in my life, things I was grateful for, and recognizing how I could improve. I was writing my experiences and goals on a daily basis; getting things off my head, which allowed me to sleep a lot better. This is powerful. When you write things on paper, magical things happen. Studies show that just by writing down your goals on a piece of paper one time, it can increase the ability to complete that goal by a rate of 50%, even if you don't read them again. I highly suggest that you write down with pen and paper versus a digital device.

#5 Pray and or Meditate: The fifth thing that most successful people do character-wise is to Pray or meditate to God, Source, the universe, or a higher power. If you don't normally pray, just talk to God throughout your day. Pretend he's just a friend you can't see but can feel him or her. Some say prayer is when you talk to God and meditation is when God talks to you. I highly believe that. I started meditating consistently not too long ago, and it has made such a difference in my life; the way I'm able to put things in perspective.

These five character traits completely changed my life. As a matter of fact, two weeks after I started doing these things on a regular basis, I had an incredible experience that transformed my life for the better. One Tuesday morning on June 14th I woke up with purpose!! I remember crying that morning. These were not tears of sadness or bitterness, but of cleansing. Tears of joy, and I knew that life was going to be incredible from then on. I knew exactly why I was here on planet earth. It was such an extraordinary experience. I felt like I was floating on clouds for many days after.

Since then, my life is more like a movie script that I have written. I feel like I'm now guided by a higher power, I feel like doors open now without effort. There are still many obstacles and personal challenges but I now have a guiding light that shines upon me. I feel blessed to find my purpose, because I wasn't even looking for it. I believe doing these 5 things on a regular basis has had much to do with it. When I feel out of "balance" it's usually because I haven't been practicing these rituals on a consistent daily basis.

▶ | **Questions**

1. What is easy to do , is also easy not to do. True or False

2. Writing things down at night can help you sleep better. True or false

3. What does success look like to you?

_____

_____

_____

_____

_____

_____

_____

_____

This is an Interactive Book with Free Videos!

Please register by visiting the website, and get instant access to **17 FREE videos** that summarize each chapter. Simply go to:

www.MidasMindsetBook.com

or scan this QR code with your smartphone.

▶ | **Notes**

▶ About the Author

Marcos Orozco is founder of Gentepeneur.com. He is a best-selling author, influential speaker and a thought leader for the fast growing Gentepreneur movement in the United States. He loves empowering his community by connecting with ambitious Latinos for exciting projects and mentoring troubled youth. An immigrant born in Nicaragua, his parents brought him and his sister to Los Angeles in the early 1980s for a chance at a brighter future. After troublesome times during his adolescence, he persevered and since then has studied some of the most successful and influential business leaders in America.

Successfully launching ventures for more than a decade, Marcos claims that the secret to his success learning from his failures. He dedicates most of his time to his son and his purpose . He is currently writing his next book "*From Ghetto to Greatness.*"

▶ Thank You

Thank you for reading my book. If you enjoyed it, please take a moment to leave me a review.

► | Connect with Me

www.Gentepreneur.com

www.MidasMindsetBook.com

www.BookLaunchAcademy.com

www.ingramcontent.com/pod-product-compliance
Lightning Source LLC
Chambersburg PA
CBHW020914180526
45163CB00007B/2727